1196
ST

DISCARD

DEMCO

The Strange World of Deep-Sea Vents

R. V. Fodor

—an Earth Processes book—

ENSLOW PUBLISHERS, INC.
Bloy St. & Ramsey Ave.　　　　P.O. Box 38
Box 777　　　　　　　　　　　Aldershot
Hillside, N.J. 07205　　　　　Hants GU12 6BP
U.S.A.　　　　　　　　　　　　U.K.

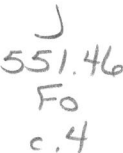

Copyright © 1991 by R.V. Fodor

All rights reserved.

No part of this book may be reproduced by any means without the written permission of the publisher.

Library of Congress Cataloging-in-Publication Data

Fodor, R. V.
    The strange world of deep-sea vents / R.V. Fodor.
       p. cm.— (an Earth Processes book)
    Includes bibliographical references.
    Summary: Explores the geology of hydrothermal vents, the life around them, and their value as a future resource.
    ISBN 0-89490-249-0
    1. Hydrothermal vents—Juvenile literature. 2. Hydrothermal vent ecology—Juvenile literature. [1. Hydrothermal vents.
2. Hydrothermal vent ecology. 3. Ecology.] I. Title. II. Series.
GB1198.F63 1991
551.46'01—dc20   89-71442
                                                                                         CIP
                                                                                          AC

Printed in the United States of America

10 9 8 7 6 5 4 3 2 1

Illustration credits:
J.P. Chanton, p. 53; J.F. Grassle, Woods Hole Oceanographic Institution, p. 28, 44; H.J. Hofmann, University of Montreal, p. 52; J.C. Holden, pp. 18, 19, 21, 22, 24, 32, 34; Institution of Scrap Iron and Steel, Washington, D.C., p. 56; D. Kamykowski, p. 40; Lamont-Doherty Geological Observatory, p. 13; L.A. Levin, pp. 6, 42; W.R. Normack, U.S. Geological Survey, pp. 29, 35, 43; Scripps Instituion of Oceanography, p. 30; Sea Education Association, p. 57; F.N. Spiess, Scripps Institution of Oceanography, pp. 9, 50; C. Wirsen, Woods Hole Oceanographic Institution, p. 7; Woods Hole Oceangraphic Institution, p. 41; U.S. Geological Survey, p. 17.

Cover photo:
U.S. Geological Survey

Contents

1 "Oases" in the Sea 5
2 Hot Water From the Cold Seafloor 15
3 Seafloor Metalworks 26
4 Colonies in the Dark 37
5 Black Smokers and the Science Ahead 49

  Glossary 58

  Further Reading 61

  Index 63

1
"Oases" in the Sea

The research ship *Knorr,* operated by Woods Hole Oceanographic Institution in Massachusetts, arrived at its destination in the eastern Pacific Ocean on February 13, 1977. The site was 200 miles (330 km) northeast of the Galapagos Islands, and the water below the *Knorr* was 1.5 miles (2.5 km) deep. Most of the people aboard were geologists, scientists who study the earth. They were in the Pacific Ocean to try to find out why an earlier 1976 scientific survey of the region had measured water temperatures near parts of the sea floor that were 10° to 15°C (20° to 30°F) warmer than the normal seafloor temperature of about 2°C (35°F).

The *Knorr* scientists planned to investigate these pockets of warm water in two ways. The first method was to tow a camera on a "sled" to photograph long stretches of sea bottom. Then they would use the photographs as a guide for diving to particular locations on the seafloor. Two geologists and a submarine pilot would visit the warm areas in a small three-person diving vessel, the U.S. Navy's submersible *Alvin*.

The Discovery
The oceanographic research began with twelve hours of sledding a

camera and strobe lights across 10 miles (16 km) of seafloor. The tow produced three thousand photographs, nearly all of which showed only ordinary barren ocean floor. Thirteen photographs, however, introduced an awesome new undersea world. They captured a field of seafloor warm springs inhabited by colonies of huge shelled animals thriving in the hot water. Such warm-water "fountains" had never been seen on the seafloor, and giant clams and mussels had never been suspected of living below the depth of sunlight penetration.

In short time, geologists John Corliss of Oregon State University and Tjeerd van Andel of Stanford University were in the *Alvin* and diving to their "clambake" discovery. Their target was smaller than the size of a baseball field. But through the help of radio signals from acoustic transponders left on the seafloor by the 1976 survey crew, the *Alvin* easily zeroed in on a Pacific warm spring.

The *Alvin* is a three-person submarine, or submersible, used to visit and explore the ocean floor.

As seen from portholes, *Alvin*'s spotlights first located water shimmering as it rose like giant curtains from every crack in the rock seafloor. By placing a flowmeter over three places that appeared to have strong vertical currents, Corliss estimated from the *Alvin* that 0.5 to 2.5 gallons (2 to 10 liters) poured out each second. A short distance above, the shimmering water turned murky as a dark "smoke" of particles fell from the plume of warm water and settled to stain the floor brown. It seemed as though minerals were forming in the mixture of warm and cold seawater and accumulating while the two scientists watched, building up thick deposits on the seafloor.

White clams up to 12 inches (30 cm) long, and huge brown mussels and white crabs nearly as large clung to the rocks around the warm spring that Corliss and van Andel floated over. As scientists, they had always believed that such animals needed sunlight to survive. This newly discovered pitch-black world centered on a warm spring

Giant clams cluster along seafloor cracks that emit streams of warm water near the Galapagos Islands, in the East Pacific Ocean.

was therefore baffling. Equally puzzling was what these creatures could possibly eat to survive in their seafloor "oasis" only 150 feet (50 m) across and over a mile below sea level.

Insight into how the undersea spring supported life began to unfold aboard the *Knorr*. When water samples collected by the *Alvin* crew were opened for study, the smell of rotten eggs poured out. That meant the water probably contained hydrogen sulfide. Could such chemicals in the hot ocean water serve as part of a food chain that existed without need for sunlight?

Temporarily setting aside the search for answers, the *Alvin* crew continued their Pacific expedition for twenty-three more dives that led to the discovery and study of three more warm-water vents. The kingdoms around each were slightly different and were given the distinguishing names Garden of Eden, Oyster Bed, and Dandelions. This last site contained animals that resembled dandelions gone to seed. The others housed white-stalked tube worms with bright-red tops and carpets of what seemed to be bacteria. The *Alvin* dives located former vent colonies, too, where all shelled and worm life was dead, apparently because the jets of warm water had shut down.

Seafloor Chimneys and Other Scientific Rewards

Since that 1977 discovery of undersea warm springs, or hydrothermal vents as geologists prefer to call them, dozens more have been located and visited in the Pacific and Atlantic oceans. Most vents blast jets of black water much hotter than the water at the first springs found. Temperatures are commonly 260° to 315°C (500° to 600°F) and over 370°C (700°F) at some. This is hot enough to melt the thermometers that measure the heat and to destroy the Plexiglas viewports in submersibles.

Hydrothermal vents are often marked by "chimneys" of rock that resemble smokestacks belching streams of black smoke. These chimneys are made of minerals that precipitate, or settle out, and accumulate where the hot water discharging from the seafloor enters cold

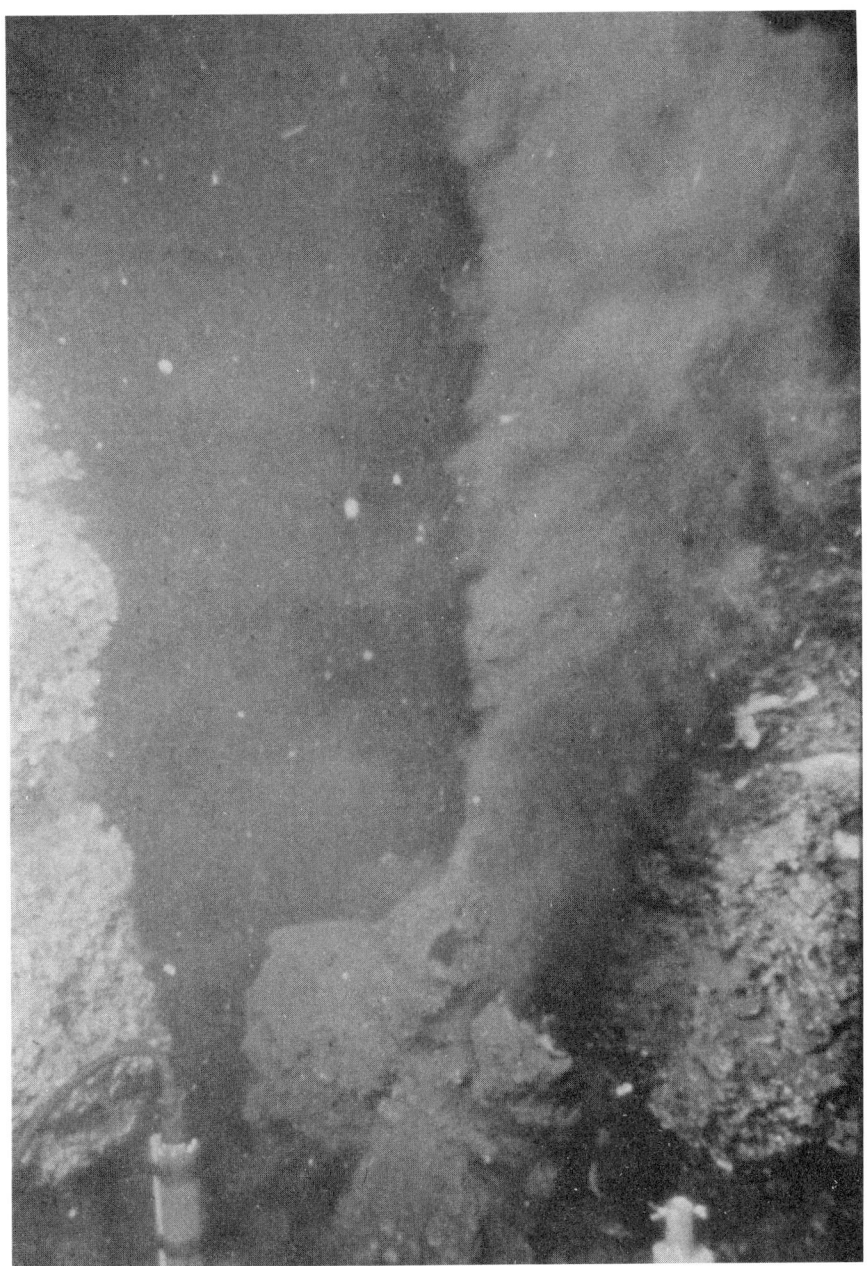

These rock chimneys, viewed from the *Alvin*, spew hot, cloudy seawater 315°C (600°F) like fire hoses on the East Pacific Ocean floor.

seawater. They are generally perched on rocky mounds about 6 to 60 feet (2 to 20 m) higher than the surrounding seafloor and about the size of a basketball court in area. The mounds, too, are made of minerals that form from the chemical reactions between normal seawater and the plume of hot water that mushrooms out above the hydrothermal vent.

The discovery and examination of black "smokers" on the seafloor has greatly advanced the geological sciences. One big reason pertains to metallic ore. The chimneys are made of the same ore minerals mined on land for iron, copper, manganese, nickel, zinc, and cadmium. Even gold and silver are in the rocks that surround vents. The chimneys gushing superhot water are actively forming deposits, or accumulations, of the same minerals humankind has used to industrialize civilization. Hydrothermal vent chimneys, therefore, represent underwater ore deposits in the making and provide geologists with new information about metal mineralization, or ore formation. Studying these rocky towers has also helped geologists to recognize certain continental rocks as originating on seafloors millions of years ago.

Seafloor vents have also rewarded biologists, the scientists who study life forms. Hydrothermal vents harbor new species of life that can survive without radiation from the sun. Vents show that certain shelled animals believed extinct for millions of years still thrive in undersea worlds far from reach. Also, the presence of certain life forms at hydrothermal vents has helped to identify some fossils in rocks on land.

Chemical and biological studies about how the vent clams, crabs, and worms survive without sunlight provide clues to how life began and how it may exist on other planets. And because vent communities are separated by tens, and sometimes hundreds, of miles, scientists have opportunities to understand how newly formed populations of life migrate to occupy new regions of the dark undersea world.

Early Studies of the Sea

Exactly when and where in history the seafloor was first explored is difficult to determine. Early scientific observations about the sea began at least as far back as 100 B.C., and probably much earlier. For example, the Greek philosopher Aristotle (384-322 B.C.) noted that the amounts of sea life decreased with increasing water depth. Aristotle based his observations on the smaller catches in fishing nets dragged through deep waters compared to nets that fished shallow waters.

More recently in history, the voyage of the British vessel H.M.S. *Challenger* marked a major turning point in understanding oceans. From 1872 to 1876, the *Challenger* scoured 68,000 miles (110,000 km) of oceans. Its scientific party hauled up 133 loads of rock and sediment and made 492 measurements, or soundings, of ocean depths by using weighted hemp lines. With samples of the bottom sediments, the crew was able to construct maps illustrating the different characteristics of the ocean floor, charting zones that have red clays, siliceous oozes, and carbonate oozes. Among the bottom samples were some apple-sized manganese nodules, the first metal recovered from an ocean floor. The life forms hauled aboard included 4,717 new animal species and proved that a variety of sea life occupied the dark abyss, contrary to common beliefs of the times. The amount of oceanographic information acquired during the *Challenger* expedition was so enormous that it took seventy-six authors twenty-three years to describe it in fifty volumes.

World Wars I and II indirectly advanced ocean-research technology. The importance of operating submarines close to shorelines and detecting enemy submarines from ships played a role in developing the echo sounder. This is a device that emits sounds toward a solid object, such as an undersea cliff. The time it takes for the sound to arrive and return, or echo, is used to calculate the distance between ship and object. Continuous soundings made by cruising ships have enabled mapping of the topography, or hills and valleys, of the entire seafloor.

Submersibles are of special interest to hydrothermal vent observations and research. Perhaps the earliest credit for using this approach for scientific studies should go to Alexander the Great (356–323 B.C.). He supposedly made a glass diving bell to explore the depths of the Aegean Sea.

From a technological point of view, America's Robert Fulton, best known for his steamboat, was among the first to develop a mechanical submarine. In France in 1800, he launched the *Nautilus* at Rouen. It was an enclosed sailing vessel about 25 feet (8 m) long that could be submerged by laying the sail and mast flat and then pumping water into a special compartment. His intention was to use the *Nautilus* to either spike or explode the underside of enemy ships. Unfortunately for Fulton, however, his experimental ship never impressed the French, British, or American governments enough for them to use it in warfare.

Modern submersibles for scientific research had their birth in the 1930s. In 1934, zoologist William Beebe and engineer Otis Barton used a tethered bathysphere, a thick-walled steel ball that was slightly less than 5 feet (1.7 m) across to descend 3,000 feet (1,000 m) off Bermuda to photograph deep-sea life. Beebe described the undersea sights through 3-inch (8-cm)-thick quartz viewports by telephone to an assistant aboard the barge *Ready*, to which he was attached by cable. His observations and the paintings based on them provided the world with its first view of the deep-sea kingdom.

Following World War II, Swiss scientist August Piccard designed the bathyscaphe *Trieste*, a submersible similar to the kind used by oceanographers today. The U.S. Navy purchased the *Trieste* in 1953 and used it in 1960 to reach 35,000 feet (10,915 m) in the Mariana trench of Guam. No submersible has since achieved that depth.

Why Study Hydrothermal Vents?

Undersea hydrothermal vents have probably existed for most of the earth's 4.65-billion-year life span. But their discovery required technology advanced to a level where temperature-sensitive instruments, cameras, and small submarines could operate and sample material in the deep ocean.

Today United States and French scientists routinely use the *Alvin*, the *Sea Cliff*, the *Cyana* (France), and similar submersibles to explore the oceans. Russian oceanographers, too, are joining the undersea efforts as demonstrated in July 1989 when a Soviet oceanographic fleet docked at Washington, D.C. These visitors from the Shirshov Institute of Oceanography came to attend the International Geological Congress and used the opportunity to show off new $25 million vessels, *Mir I* and *Mir II*, that can dive as deep as 4 miles (6 km) and remain on the ocean bottom 20 hours.

Of all the discoveries oceanographers have made, none has excited the scientific communities more than black smokers in the

An oceanographer launches a bathythermograph from the research vessel *Conrad* to determine water temperatures at different depths.

"oases" of the sea. Geologists are using information about these features to learn more about how mineral deposits form and where to find ore on both land and in the sea. Vents have stimulated dreams of developing technology for the future mining of underwater riches. Vents also provide information about the geologic processes involved in the earth's tectonic movements that make new ocean floors, destroy old ones, and separate the continents.

Chemical oceanographers are learning what is responsible for the composition of seawater and how it changes over time and from one place to another. Physical oceanographers can use the chemical signatures of hydrothermal vents to help trace patterns and rates of deep water flow. And biologists are learning about the origin and evolution of life forms and how certain ones adapt to and reproduce in hostile environments.

Foremost, however, is the question of why there are hydrothermal vents at all. What is special about certain areas of the seafloor where hot water jets out from cracks, bringing ingredients to make mineral deposits and to sustain animal communities that do not need sunlight?

2
Hot Water From the Cold Seafloor

Nearly 6,000 years had passed since Helgafell volcano had last erupted to flood the Icelandic island of Heimaey with molten rock. When it did reawaken on January 23, 1973, it opened a mile-long (1.6-km) fracture in the earth's crust to spit out lava as a fiery "curtain." For two days, the 5,300 residents of this island in the North Atlantic Ocean watched in awe as the lava accumulated but kept its distance from their homes.

Island of Fire

After a few days, lava stopped shooting from the fracture, and the eruption focused to construct a single cone of cinders and spattering lava. The cone quickly grew to 300 feet (100 m) tall. Black cinders exploding from the cone gradually buried roofs and roads, and Heimaey residents evacuated to Iceland 6 miles (10 km) away. Of greater concern than sooty towns, however, was that lava continued to flow slowly from the volcanic cone. It threatened to destroy the harbor and the fishing port that Icelanders considered to be their country's best.

Weeks passed as the displaced people waited for the eruption to end, and the lava flow continued its journey from the cone to the harbor. It moved sluggishly, resembling a stream of molasses, but was hotter than the inside of a blast furnace. By March, the molten rock had covered homes, a fish-processing plant, and a power plant. Emergency action against the lava was necessary if Heimaey could ever again support a population and its businesses.

Because there were no known ways of stopping lava, any attempt to do so would be experimental. The most reasonable idea was to pump cold seawater from the harbor onto the surface of the lava. If the lava temperature could be reduced from its normal 1,100°C (2,000°F) to about 1,000°C (1,800°F), it would begin to harden into rock. This would create wall-like barriers that would retard the advancement of new lava coming from the cone.

It took weeks to arrange for the cooling experiment, but by April, forty-seven water pumps mounted on barges occupied the harbor. The pumps turned water directly on the 100 foot (35 m) thick lava front, which was then at sea level and about to enter the harbor. Elsewhere, a network of plumbing resembling an irrigation operation squirted seawater over the surface of the flow as far as a mile from the harbor.

Results came slowly. It took two weeks to cool enough of the molten rock to create barriers and save the harbor. Finally, in June, the volcanic activity quieted and threats of destruction ended.

The 1973 Helgafell eruption was the fourth volcanic eruption for Icelanders within ten years, and about the hundredth since Iceland was settled in A.D. 874. One recent episode gave birth to an island. In 1963 a volcano sprang up practically overnight from beneath 425 feet (125 m) of water. It remains today as Surtsey, about a mile across and located 20 miles (33 km) from Iceland.

An Undersea Mountain Range

Iceland is a nation of volcanoes, geysers, and hot springs. Practically every part of Iceland had its origin as lava. The country exists because so much volcanism, or volcanic activity, occurred on the North Atlantic

Ocean floor during the past 50 million years that lava piled high above sea level. It created an island the size of the state of Georgia.

But Iceland is only one of many sites of ocean-floor volcanism. Iceland belongs to a monstrous submarine mountain range made of a string of volcanoes and the lava they erupted. In the Atlantic, this volcanic range is called the Mid-Atlantic ridge. It is one segment of an ocean-floor range that spans the globe nearly continuously for 40,000 miles (65,000 km). Geologists refer to this global range as the midocean ridge system, even though some parts are not in the middle of an ocean.

The entire ridge system is volcanic, but at any one time only portions are steaming with hot springs or molten rock. Exactly where

Fire hoses douse the encroaching lava from Helgafell volcano in an attempt to freeze its advance.

these geologic processes occur along the midocean ridge changes with time. However, wherever volcanism or hot springs do exist along the ridge, magma is churning below. Magma is molten rock that rises from depths inside the earth from about 6 to 60 miles (10 to 100 km). It is almost always hotter than 1,100°C (2,000°F). Before erupting, magma usually resides in large reservoirs in the crust. These reservoirs are generally at shallow depths, only a few miles or less. After it erupts onto the surface, geologists often refer to magma as lava.

Scientists were not surprised, then, that the first warm springs in the ocean were discovered near the Galapagos Islands in the Pacific. That region contains the part of the midocean ridge system called the East Pacific rise. This geologic feature represents millions of years of magma erupting to form volcanoes and, in the process, adding new rock to the Pacific Ocean floor. Geologists had suspected that seawater

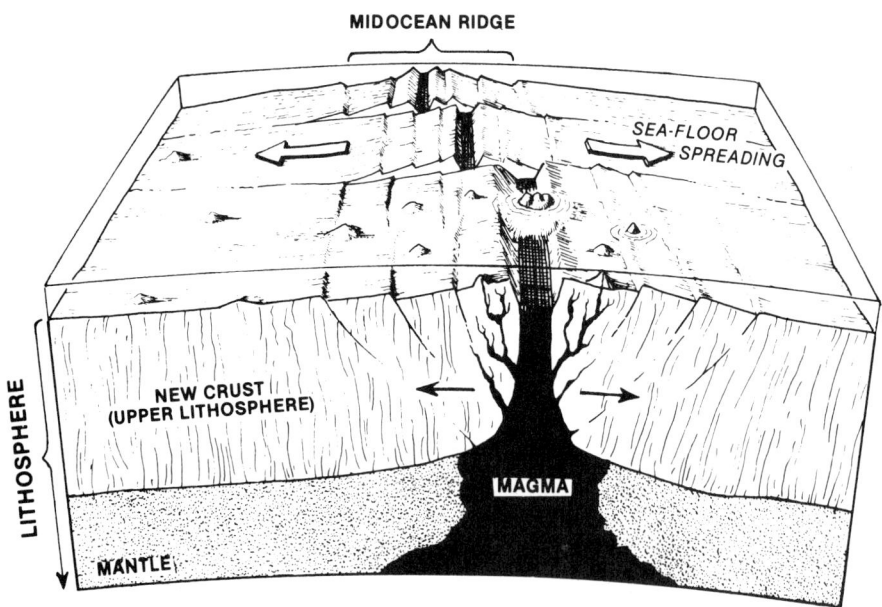

Magma erupts along the midocean ridge system. It sometimes erupts in enough quantity to form volcanoes and volcanic islands. When magma cools to rock, it forms new ocean floor. As the midocean ridge spreads apart in opposite directions, more magma rises to fill the gap.

probably sinks into ocean-floor cracks near eruption sites such as the East Pacific rise, and that heat from the magma reservoirs below would warm the seawater far above its normal temperature. This process would create hot springs.

The Concept of Plate Tectonics

Explanations of why a submarine mountain range straddles the earth and why it has vents of hot water can be found in the scientific concept called plate tectonics. The word *plate* refers to the earth's outer rock layer, the lithosphere, made of several huge individual segments. The lithospheric plates are assembled like jigsaw-puzzle pieces. *Tectonics* indicates that these plates are in motion, moving apart from one another in some areas and toward one another in others.

The plates are about 60 miles (100 km) thick and usually thousands of miles across. These giant slabs of rock move slowly across the globe, traveling ½ to 6 inches (1 to 15 cm) a year—about the speed at which fingernails grow. Where lithospheric plates move

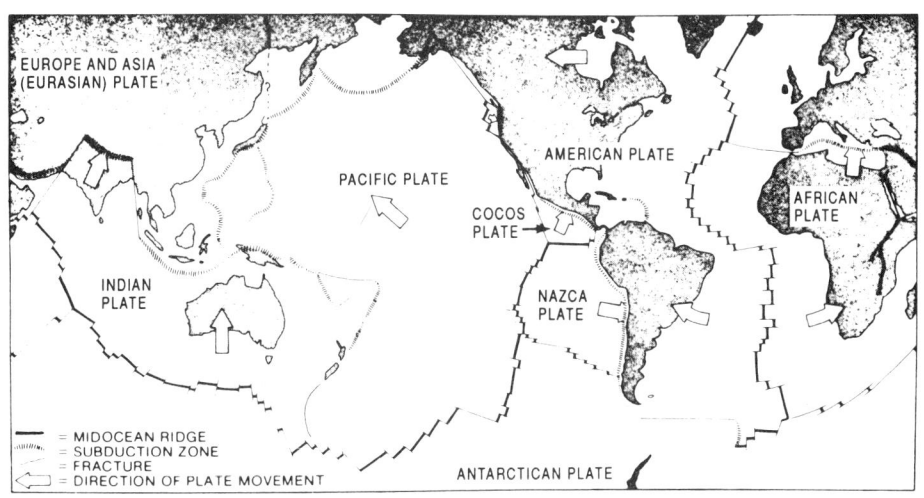

The earth's lithosphere, or outer shell, is broken into several large "plates" that slowly move in various directions a few inches per year. Spreading centers, such as the East Pacific rise and the Mid-Atlantic ridge, form where the plates move apart.

ma rises to fill the gap between. When that magma cools to ck, it forms new ocean floor. If enormous amounts of pour out, the accumulation can rise above sea level to create an island such as Iceland. Few places between the lithospheric plates, however, have erupted enough magma to form islands. But enough volcanism has occurred everywhere between the earth's lithospheric plates to develop the mountainous midocean ridge system below sea level.

The concept of plate tectonics also claims that as ocean floor is created in one region of the earth, it is destroyed elsewhere. Destruction of lithosphere happens where plates meet, or collide. One slab is forced beneath the other, or is subducted. A good example of subduction occurs where the floor of the eastern Pacific Ocean meets the South American plate. Here the Pacific floor is subducted beneath South America. Geologists point out that deep trenches in the crust, such as the Mariana trench near the Philippines and the Peru-Chile trench along South America, mark some of the earth's subduction zones.

The Creation of "Smokers"

Volcanism along the midocean ridge occurs between two plates in a narrow belt about 6 miles (10 km) wide. The volcanic rock, or new ocean crust, that forms in this "spreading center" gradually moves away as part of each plate. As the new crust departs from the direct heat of the spreading center, it cools and develops fractures from contraction during cooling. Within a few miles from a spreading center, ocean crust is likely to be riddled with a network of deep-penetrating fractures. The combined processes of crustal migration, cooling, and fracturing are often accompanied by still another geologic process. Movements of crust along the deep cracks produce mild earthquakes, but they are usually too far from land to be felt.

Collectively, the fractures form channelways that allow seawater to seep downward and become heated by magma below and expand.

High pressure at these depths below sea level, however, prevents boiling. Instead, the water remains in its liquid state and reaches temperatures greater than 390°C (700°F). At these temperatures, the hydrothermal solutions, as the heated seawater is called, are less dense than the surrounding rock. Buoyancy causes the hydrothermal solutions to stop seeping downward and to rise and exit through spreading-center passageways. The superheated waters may blast from a pipelike or geyserlike opening at velocities up to 6 feet (2 m) per second.

Where hydrothermal solutions escape in a strong vertical current, rock chimneys, or smokers, commonly form. Because of the fractured nature of the midocean ridge, however, the heated seawater may exit with less velocity from cracks and not form rock chimneys.

Thus the ocean crust near midocean ridges behaves as a giant plumbing system that recirculates water. It permits seawater to sink toward magma reservoirs, become superheated, rise, and then dis-

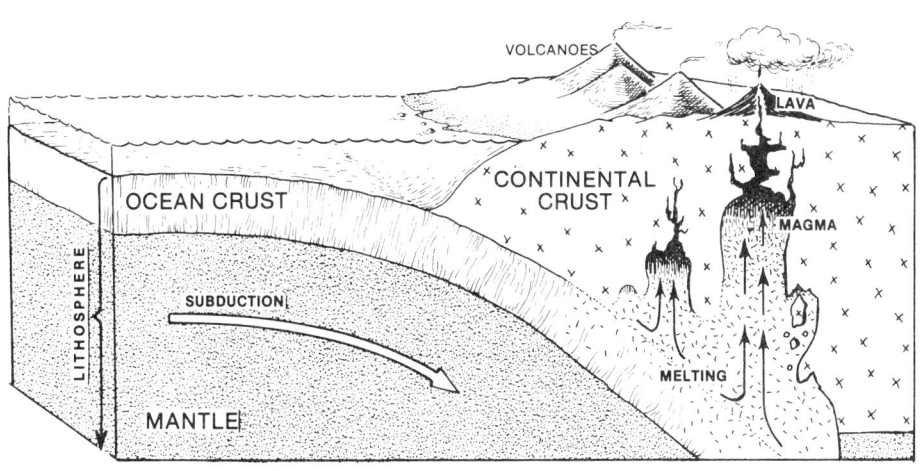

Where plates collide, such as where an ocean plate meets a continental plate, one plate passes beneath the other, or is subducted. Magma and volcanoes commonly form above subduction zones.

charge through local sites on the seafloor. Geologists call these discharging sites hydrothermal vents. Seafloor vents operate in much the same way as geysers on land, such as Old Faithful in Yellowstone National Park. In the case of geysers, however, magma reservoirs heat groundwater that has seeped downward through deep cracks in continental or island crust.

Clusters and Fields of Seafloor Vents

The reservoirs of magma below the ocean floor that occasionally erupt to form volcanic rock (new ocean crust) may be miles across in size. Like furnaces in the lithosphere, they can heat large volumes of seawater and force it up through a maze of passageways to resurface. Clusters of rock chimneys on the ocean floor mark places where heated seawater empties from the plumbing system. The chimneys stand 10 to 60 feet (3 to 20 m) above the seafloor, and those in a particular

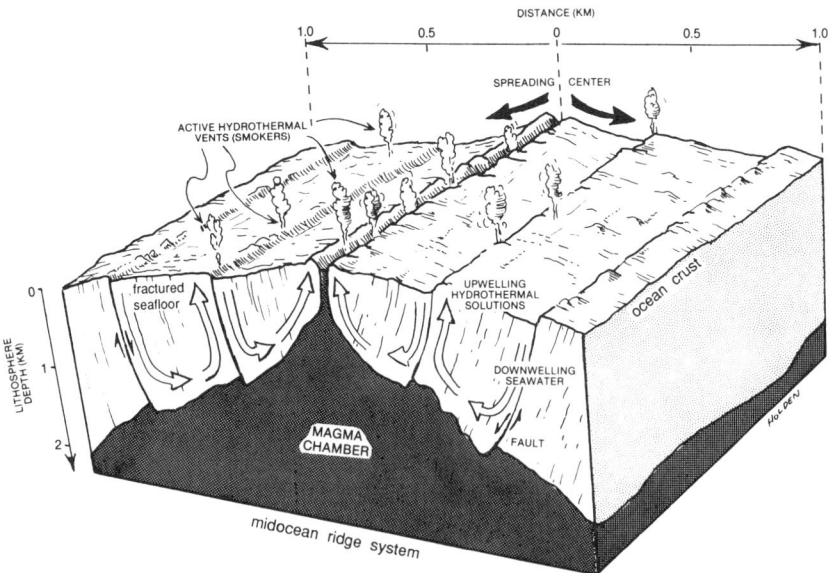

Midocean ridge "plumbing". Ocean crust forms, moves away, cools, and fractures. The fractures act as channelways through which cold seawater sinks and becomes heated. The hot water rises through other fractures to eventually escape as hydrothermal solutions that mix with cold seawater.

cluster may be spaced tens of feet apart. A second or third cluster of jetting chimneys may be only a few hundred feet away. If several vent clusters are within one area, they define a hydrothermal field. A stretch of midocean ridge a few miles long may contain many fields. They all may be heated by a single gigantic magma reservoir below.

The temperatures of hydrothermal solutions shooting from a chimney depend partly on how close the seawater seeping downward comes to magma heat before turning to rise and escape. Exit temperatures also vary with the amount of downward-moving cold seawater that mixes with the rising solutions. This mixing occurs in crustal fractures during the upward journey from heat source to ocean floor. And then upon exiting a vent, of course, hydrothermal solutions mix with surrounding seawater and become cooler and more diluted with distance from the vent.

Because magma reservoirs are the engines that drive hydrothermal vents, the lifetime of a seafloor vent is linked to the life span of the magma providing heat. Magma reservoirs eventually cool and harden into rock. The overlying vents that they supplied then become extinct, and the surrounding sea life dies. Another sure death for a hydrothermal vent occurs when the plumbing system feeding it becomes clogged and hot water can no longer escape through that passage. Faulting, the movement of blocks of ocean crust along deep fractures, is one way that plumbing becomes plugged up in one area and opens in another.

Hotspots and Hot Vents

Not all magma reservoirs below the ocean floor are located beneath the midocean ridge. Geologists recognize about one hundred additional "hotspots" within lithospheric plates and away from plate margins. The Hawaiian Islands, located in the middle of a plate, are the best example. This island chain formed because the Pacific plate slowly passes over a deep heat source that has continuously provided magma for at least 70 million years.

Dr. Alexander Malahoff, a University of Hawaii marine geologist, was among those who began underwater studies of the Hawaiian hotspot in the early 1980s. Among his research objectives was to determine if the Hawaiian hotspot would create yet another island in the future. Using bottom-survey photography, and magnetic-field and temperature measurements, Malahoff detected a new volcano growing about 25 miles (40 km) from the island of Hawaii. Called Loihi submarine volcano, it is over a mile tall and within a half-mile (and probably thousands of years) of emerging from the sea as an island.

During the scientific surveys, water-temperature measurements of certain areas directly above Loihi volcano showed the seafloor to be several degrees warmer than expected. This gave Malahoff and his fellow oceanographers the clues that Loihi, too, had vents for hydrothermal solutions. Photographs of fresh lava flows and rock

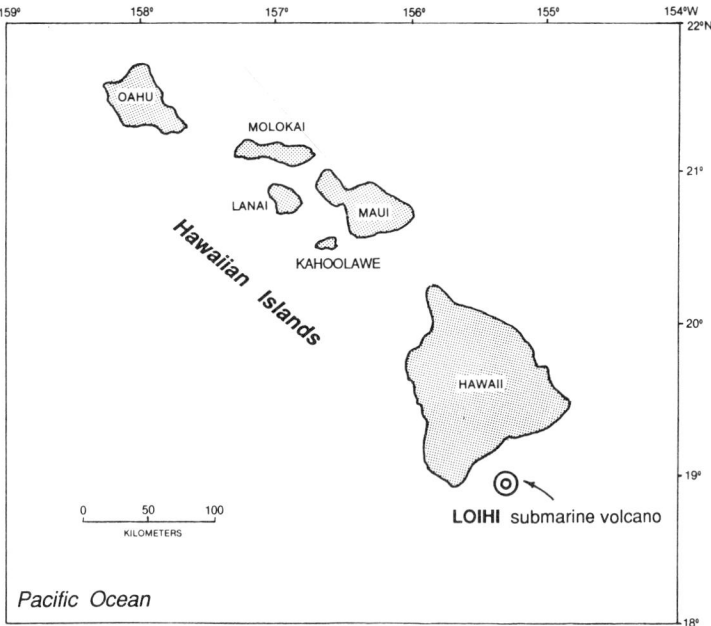

Loihi submarine volcano is forming from the same hotspot that created the Hawaiian Islands.

chimneys gave the proof that magma at depth was both erupting to make new ocean crust and heating seawater that had seeped downward through cracks.

When the *Alvin* dove to Loihi in 1987, it photographed small organisms floating and surviving in the 30°C (86°F) water above chimneys in two fields that the geologists named Pele's vents and Kapo's vents. The chimneys were large, nearly 100 feet (30 m) high, but no giant clams or worms were found in the surrounding areas. Malahoff believes that their absence means that Loihi is too isolated and too young for large sea life forms to have located it and established colonies. Metals, however, are present. Studies since those first visits show Loihi vent rocks to contain iron, manganese, cobalt, copper, chromium, zinc, nickel, and gold.

Metal accumulations are features common to all vents—whether on a midocean ridge or on Loihi. Because we mine metals on land for use in our daily lives, scientists want to study the minerals of seafloor rock chimneys and the surrounding mounds. Evaluations are made of the metal-bearing minerals both on the seafloor and in the laboratory. Much of the scientific interest lies in finding out what is special about hydrothermal vents that enables metals to accumulate there. Exactly what conditions are necessary for metal formation, and is this how all the valuable metal deposits on earth were formed?

3
Seafloor Metalworks

The floor of the Gulf of California seemed an unlikely place to find mineral deposits. It is blanketed by mud hundreds of feet thick. These sediments gradually collected in this narrow body of seawater over the past three million years from the erosion of neighboring land—Baja California and mainland Mexico.

But geologists had acquired several clues that metals formed part of the Gulf of California seafloor. Measurements of bottom temperatures taken during surveys in the 1970s revealed places that were hot. Scientists interpreted these hot zones as places where hydrothermal solutions discharged from fractured seafloor crust. Also, below the sediments, they knew, was a portion of the midocean ridge system known as the East Pacific rise. And geologists recognized this plate-tectonic feature elsewhere as containing both hot-water vents and deposits of metal-bearing minerals.

There was another sign that the floor of the Gulf of California probably contained metals. It was a high-temperature geothermal field located in southern California where the East Pacific rise extends beneath land. Magma Power Company had been using the heat from this Salton Sea geothermal operation to generate electricity. A peculiar thing about this energy source, however, was that deposits of copper and silver minerals regularly plugged the piping used to extract heat. Their source was hydrothermal solutions circulating in the California crust.

Metals in a Muddy Seafloor

In 1980, the research vessel *Melville* entered the Gulf of California with geologists planning to precisely locate the warm areas and to sample any nearby rock. Earlier expeditions had dredged some rocks and cored mud but had not recovered any metal-bearing minerals. The *Melville* crew, however, was better prepared. They used the Scripps Institution of Oceanography's *Deep Tow* vehicle to map and photograph a 75 square-mile (190 square-km) area along the valley that marked the axis of the East Pacific rise. Within only days, its sonars located dozens of rock structures protruding above the muddy bottom.

Knowing exactly where to look, then, geologists like Peter Lonsdale, a researcher at Scripps Institution of Oceanography, began dredging the seafloor with a chain basket lowered from the ship. Other samples of the seafloor were acquired by coring the mud to 30 foot (10 m) depths. Results showed the gulf to be rich in metal. Sulfide minerals containing zinc, copper, iron, and lead comprised the rocks captured in the dredge basket. The cored muds had veins of metal-bearing minerals created by the passage of hot fluids through narrow channels.

Higher temperatures at greater depths into the seafloor also suggested the presence of hydrothermal solutions. Lonsdale measured a 4°C (7°F) rise with each additional yard of depth into the mud. By 30 feet (10 m) down, it was hotter than 100°C (210°F), or enough to melt the plastic liner of the sediment corer.

Two years passed before scientists dove in the *Alvin* to visit the Gulf of California vent fields. That expedition showed the visitors black smokers spewing hydrothermal solutions and thickets of tubeworms, giant clams, and fluffy mats of bacteria surrounding the vents. Samples of the seafloor chimneys proved most rewarding. In terms of mineral deposits, these columnar structures were identified as "massive sulfides." That is, the chimneys were made almost entirely of sulfur-bearing minerals that contained metals in quantities thousands of times greater than in ordinary seafloor rock and seawater. For example, laboratory analyses of the vent mineral sphalerite showed it to contain about 45 percent zinc, 20 percent iron, 34 percent sulfur, and small amounts of manganese and cadmium. As one comparison, volcanic rock and seawater contain almost no zinc.

Seafloor Vent Metals: A Common Occurrence?

By the mid-1980s, when reports of the Gulf of California vents were finally published, the community of earth scientists was no longer surprised about the "polymetallic" (containing many metals) composition of hydrothermal vents. By then, enough seafloor vents had been

Samples of these rocks from a hydrothermal vent field on the East Pacific Ocean floor proved to be rich in metal sulfide minerals.

discovered and examined so that researchers expected metal deposits wherever hydrothermal solutions mixed with cold seawater. In addition to those in the gulf, there were discoveries of rich zinc, copper, and iron deposits on the East Pacific rise at the mouth of the gulf at 21° N latitude. Hydrothermal fields had also been found on the northern Mid-Atlantic ridge; these contained manganese oxide. And three vents sampled by *Alvin* crews on the Juan de Fuca ridge offshore from Washington State had abundant sphalerite and the copper mineral chalcopyrite.

The discoveries continue today. Dr. Peter Rona of the National Oceanographic and Atmospheric Administration in Miami, Florida, and his scientific staff made one of the more recent observations. Using the U.S. Navy's Deep Submergence Vehicle *Sea Cliff* between September 15-30, 1988, they found a hydrothermal field several

Scientists in the *Alvin* can retrieve rock samples by using a mechanical arm.

hundred meters long on the Gorda ridge. The location of the Sea Cliff hydrothermal field—named after the submersible—is 125 miles (200 km) offshore from Oregon in water depths of 8,000 feet (2,700 m).

Seafloor investigations in recent years had noted, too, that most ridge vents contained nonmetallic minerals. The hot fluids had also formed minerals such as barite, which contains barium, and anhydrite, a calcium-sulfur mineral. Quartz, a common mineral on land made of silicon and oxygen, is also present.

If hydrothermal solutions began as ordinary seawater, scientists wondered, how did they deposit minerals rich in metal when escaping from the seafloor to recirculate in the sea? The explanation, geologists have found, is in certain chemical reactions. These begin below the seafloor where the hot seawater is in close contact with the crustal rock it passes through; the reactions end where the heated water enters the

The U.S. Navy's *Sea Cliff* submersible helped locate hydrothermal vents offshore from Oregon and Washington states.

cold seawater at the vents. But understanding exactly what these undersea chemical reactions produce requires knowledge about minerals.

Atoms Combine to Make Minerals

Geologists recognize that all matter, including minerals, is made of atoms of elements, such as oxygen, hydrogen, iron, and aluminum. Atoms of one element usually occur in some combination with atoms of other elements. Lead atoms may bond with sulfur to form lead sulfide, for example, and tin atoms may combine with oxygen to form tin oxide. Additionally, some metal atoms occur in pure form without other elements. Native gold and native copper are examples.

Atoms that pack together may make up a mineral, so long as the atoms do not represent organic material. This means that animal and plant life cannot be included as minerals. Minerals are inorganic material.

The atoms of the various elements in minerals are combined in particular proportions. This gives each mineral a definite chemical composition. The atoms are also in orderly arrangements, which gives each mineral a particular atomic, or physical, structure.

Halite, common table salt, offers a good illustration of what defines a mineral. Halite is made of the elements sodium and chlorine, and the atoms of each are arranged at the corners of cubes. These cube forms represent halite's internal structure, one sodium atom alternating with one chlorine atom. The cube shapes of salt grains are visible with the aid of a magnifying lens. The one-to-one proportion of sodium to chlorine atoms also gives halite its special chemical composition, sodium chloride.

About 3 percent of seawater is the ingredients of salts such as halite. When seawater evaporates, then, it leaves behind halite as solid matter. But metals are a very small part of seawater. A metal such as zinc, for instance, is only about one part of a trillion parts of seawater. On the other hand, if seawater can deposit metal, as shown by the black smokers of the sea, it must have a special source where it acquires metal atoms such as zinc, copper, and lead. The rock making up the ocean crust serves as this source.

Hot Seawater Captures Metal Atoms

Seawater passing through rock fractures and pores is able to leach, or remove, metal atoms. This means that small amounts of metal atoms already in crustal rock can be gathered and carried off to accumulate elsewhere. At least three special conditions are necessary for seawater to accomplish this leaching process—heat, salinity (saltiness), and acidity.

Seawater leaches metal atoms most efficiently from rock when it is hot. This is similar to the way that hot water removes dirt from hands or clothes better than cold water. The higher the temperature, the more easily seawater dissolves metal from rock. Underwater pressure of

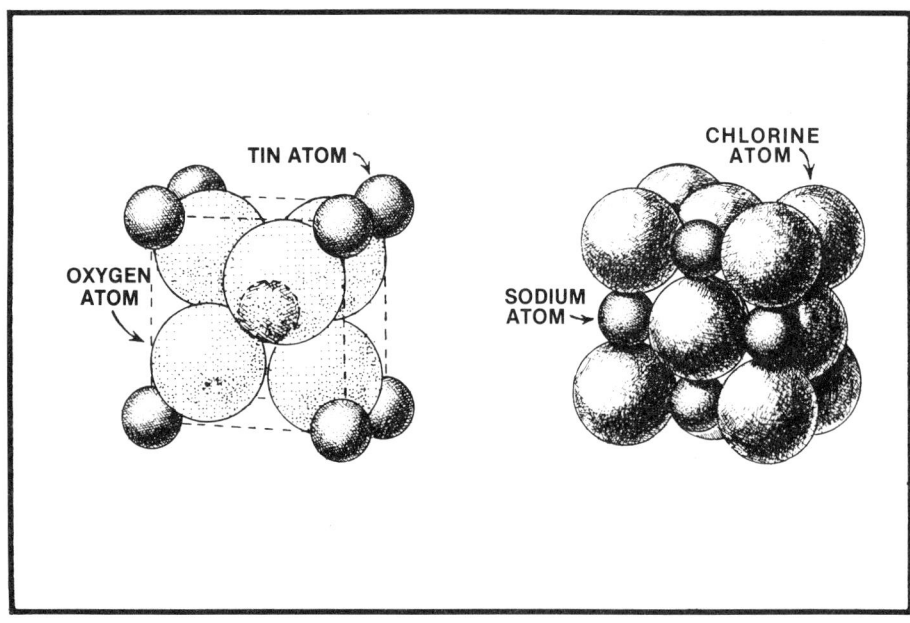

Different combinations of certain atoms, such as tin and oxygen, make up minerals that provide metals. Table salt, or halite, is a mineral made of an orderly arrangement of sodium and chlorine atoms.

more than a ton per square inch of seafloor helps, too. Pressure aids dissolving and keeping metal in saline (salty) solutions.

The salt content of seawater makes hydrothermal fluids more effective than fresh water in removing metal from rock. The reason is that dissolved salt in seawater provides abundant chlorine atoms. Metal atoms readily combine with chlorine to travel in solution as, for instance, molecules of iron chloride and zinc chloride.

Finally, laboratory experiments have shown that heated seawater becomes a mild acid. Because metals are quick to dissolve in acid, high temperatures at midocean ridges make seawater corrosive and effective in removing metal atoms from the rock it passes through.

For hydrothermal solutions to eventually deposit their dissolved metals quickly and abundantly, conditions must change to the opposite from those for dissolving metal. Hydrothermal solutions venting into cold bottom waters accomplish this. A comparison might be how a flowing river, such as the Mississippi, drops its sediment load when it enters a large, still body of water, such as the Gulf of Mexico.

When hot, metal-bearing solutions enter normal seawater of 2°C (35°F) temperature, they cool and become less saline and less acidic. Finding the new environment unfavorable for keeping metals dissolved, the solutions immediately precipitate a black "smoke" of zinc, copper, and iron atoms that combine with sulfur originally in seawater to form sulfide minerals. Where elements such as barium, calcium, and silica are abundant in the solutions, portions of the "smoke" may be white due to formation of the minerals barite, anhydrite, and quartz.

Building Chimneys

The black smoke at seafloor vents, therefore, is a cloud of dust-sized sulfide minerals. Up to 200 pounds (90 kg) of metal-bearing sulfides may exit from a chimney each day. These suspended particles travel one of several paths. Bottom currents may carry them away from the vents and far from the midocean ridge. They then become lost in the ocean waters and sediments. Alternatively, the sulfide particles accumulate directly at the vent to build a rock "chimney." Or they rain down to accumulate around the vent as a mound of sulfide minerals.

Vent chimneys begin growing soon after hot solutions first escape from a new crack in the seafloor. The fluids mix their high calcium content with the sulfate (sulfur plus oxygen) in normal seawater to crystallize the mineral anhydrite. This combination of calcium and sulfate creates a short rocky cylinder, or chimney, around the seep in the seafloor.

Thereafter, the continuing stream of fluids jetting through the new anhydrite chimney is protected from rapid mixing with seawater. But

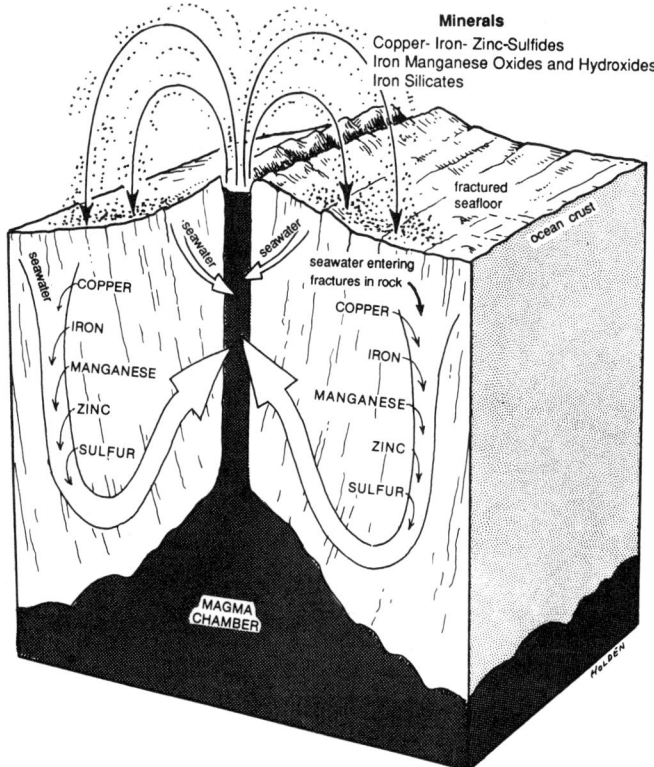

As seawater penetrates crust, it becomes heated and able to extract metals from the rock. The hot waters transport these metals up to the sea. Upon mixing with cold seawater, the hot solutions precipitate the metals as various metallic minerals that then "rain" down on the surrounding seafloor.

its contact with cold waters and the change in chemical environment are enough to grow sulfide particles inside the chimney. The metal sulfides grow as a vertical structure that may reach 30 feet (10 m) or more. Tall growth is not assured, however. The steady buildup of metal-bearing minerals can eventually clog a vent, causing it to shut down or to force new openings from the walls.

Scientists who have made multiple dives to particular vents have noted that chimneys can add several inches to their height in one day. On the other hand, seafloor chimneys may not survive long, perhaps only a few years. When one smoker on the East Pacific rise was revisited six months after the first observation in 1979, it was no longer active.

Once dead, chimneys are vulnerable to destruction by bottom

The *Alvin* sampling basket contains a large chimney fragment to examine for metal content.

currents and chemical attack. They eventually crumble and fall to the surrounding mounds of minerals and large shelled animals.

Over the life span of a vent, temperatures of escaping solutions may range from extremely hot, over 350°C (600°F) to only warm, about 25°C (70°F) or less. Temperatures, as pointed out earlier, depend partly on the amount of mixing between hydrothermal solutions and cold seawater beneath the seafloor before the solutions escape.

Lifeforms do not live directly in the hottest jets, of course. They occupy the surrounding seafloor where the mixture of hydrothermal solutions and ordinary seawater makes a mild environment, or where the seawater is an ordinary 2° to 3°C (36° to 38°F). Some habitats may be along cracks in the seafloor neighboring chimneys where only mild-temperature and not hot solutions are escaping. The warmth of the vent regions, plus chemicals distributed by the water jets, provides a home for a variety of marine life, many kinds never seen in sunlit waters.

4
Colonies in the Dark

The scientific understanding that sunlight is necessary to support life began about 350 years ago with simple experiments on plants. The Dutch chemist van Helmont reached the first milestone in 1648 with his investigation of plant growth. Van Helmont planted a 5 pound (2 kg) willow twig in a pot containing exactly 200 pounds of soil and regularly watered it for five years. Attempting to determine how much soil was used during tree growth, he protected the soil pot from gaining weight from dust. At the end of five years, the willow had grown into a small tree that weighed 164 pounds (75 kg). But the soil had lost only 2 ounces (56 g). It appeared, then, that water alone accounted for the increased size and weight of the willow—even though the tree was made of solid matter.

About one hundred years later, in 1754, Swiss naturalist Charles Bonnet demonstrated that plant leaves submerged in water slowly emitted bubbles. The plants expelled a gas—now known to be oxygen. But the bubbling, Bonnet reported, required sunlight, because it did not occur after dusk.

In 1779, the Dutch physician Jean Ingen-Housz improved upon this observation by noting that plants not only exhaled oxygen but inhaled carbon dioxide as well. This was opposite from the breathing of animals, which inhale oxygen and expel carbon dioxide. Particularly important, however, was that the exchange of carbon dioxide for oxygen by plants occurred only in sunlight. And the brighter the sunlight, the more active the exchange process.

Sunlight: Essential for Life

These early discoveries built the foundation for understanding photosynthesis, the biologic process by which plants utilize sunlight to make matter and grow. With sunlight, plants produce a chemical reaction between carbon dioxide and water to create cells of hydrocarbons (solid matter of combined hydrogen and carbon atoms) and release oxygen as gas. As a chemical process, photosynthesis can be expressed as:

$$CO_2 + H_2O + \text{sunlight and green plant} \rightarrow O_2 + \text{organic matter (hydrocarbons)}$$

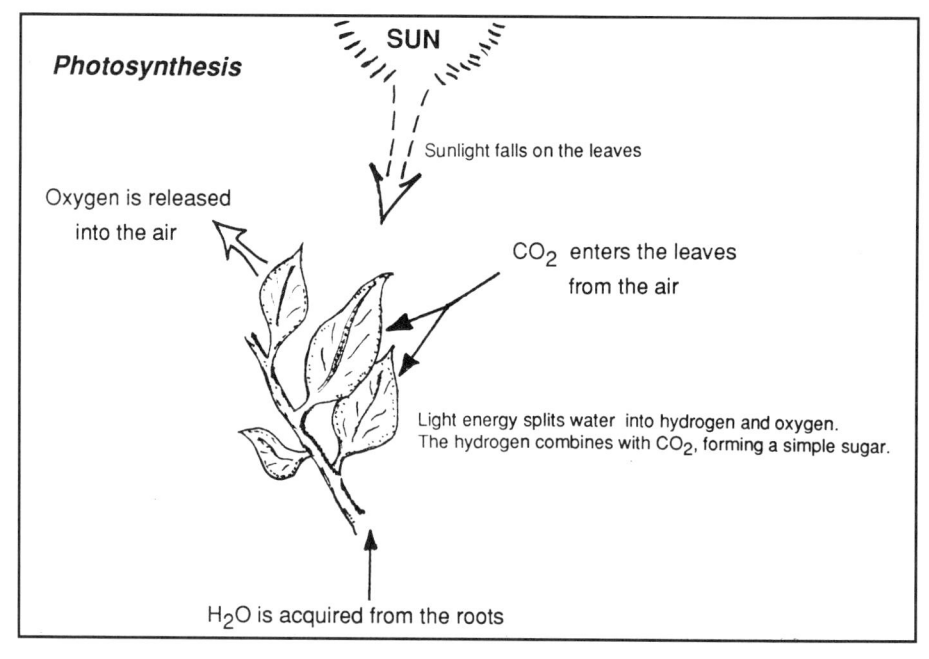

Photosynthesis

- Sunlight falls on the leaves
- Oxygen is released into the air
- CO_2 enters the leaves from the air
- Light energy splits water into hydrogen and oxygen. The hydrogen combines with CO_2, forming a simple sugar.
- H_2O is acquired from the roots

Using sunlight as an energy source, plants produce a chemical reaction to create cells and grow.

It explains that the weight gain of the tree in van Helmont's experiment was due to photosynthesis. That is, the tree grew by extracting hydrogen from water in the soil and carbon dioxide from the air to make plant material. The soil did not have to contribute much of its ingredients.

Plants, therefore, grow and survive because they store the energy of sunlight in the form of chemical energy. Animals, in contrast, grow by eating plants, or by eating animals that eat plants. In one way or another, then, all life appears to need the sun for survival.

This applies to marine life, too, even though the sun does not penetrate below about 300 feet (100 m) of water depth. In the sea, the floating small animals and plants known as plankton, such as algae, live near the surface and play a vital role in marine photosynthesis. Phytoplankton (plant plankton) forms the base of the food chain by its ability to synthesize organic carbon from carbon dioxide, water, and sunlight. But because plankton serves as food for other sea life, very little escapes consumption in shallow, lighted waters to fall to the deep sea floor to become food there.

The sparse food supply is perhaps the main reason why so few living things occur in the deep sea. It is puzzling, then, how large colonies of clams, mussels, and tubeworms live at hydrothermal vents. Their domain is in water nearly 2 miles (3 km) deep and in temperatures 4° to 38°C (40° to 100°F). It is without sunlight to provide hydrocarbons for food, and the organisms receive far too little food falling from surface waters to support their large numbers and sizes. The explanation, it turned out, of how animals thrive in this kind of hostile environment had been available to science for about a hundred years.

Useful Bacteria

By the 1800s, with the understanding of photosynthesis, scientists identified the organisms that live by photosynthesis as photo-autotrophic. This means self-supporting with the help of light.

Animals, including man, live by consuming other live or dead organisms, or organic food, and are heterotrophic.

In Paris in 1887, Serge Winogradski observed through experiments with bacteria that there was another category of organisms able to grow without sunlight and without eating other organisms. Working with a variety of bacterium known as *Beggiatoa,* Winogradski discovered that these simple life forms could synthesize organic carbon from carbon dioxide when in a hydrogen sulfide and carbon dioxide environment. That is, the bacteria transformed hydrogen sulfide into sulfur and sulfate (sulfur combined with oxygen), using the energy released to make organic carbon in the process. *Beggiatoa* grew in the dark by the chemical oxidation of hydrogen sulfide, or by chemosynthesis. They are chemoautotrophic organisms.

Because all large life forms seemed to depend on photosynthesis, there was not much scientific interest in chemosynthesis in the century after Winogradski's time. But this changed with the discovery of dense undersea populations of marine life at hydrothermal vents. Sunlight is absent at the vents, but water samples with a rotten-egg stench indicate

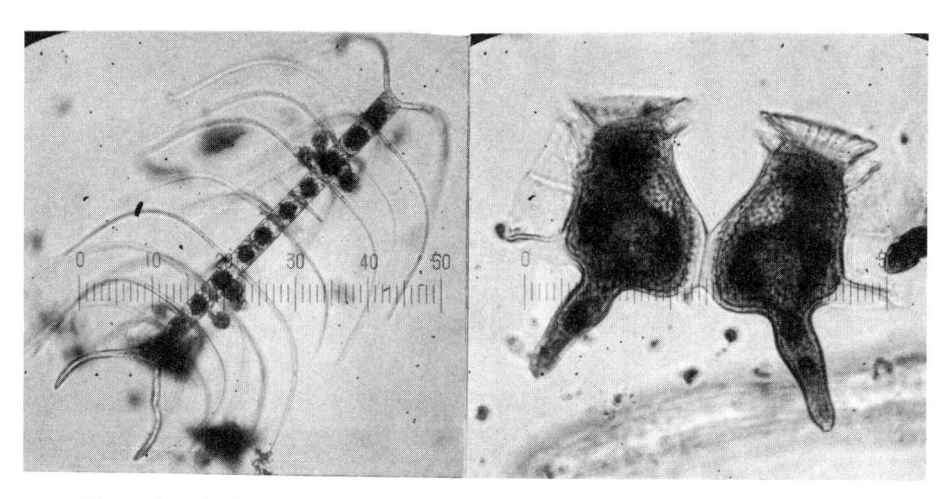

These tiny plankton, *Chaetoceros* (left) and *Dinophysis candata v.* pedunculata (right), are a food source for other marine life.

abundant hydrogen sulfide escaping from the vents—ideal conditions for chemosynthesis. Seawater provides ample carbon dioxide for the process.

Moreover, photographs and samples of undersea vents show mats of bacteria surrounding the vents, and there have been observations of vent animals directly feeding, or grazing, on the bacteria mats. Chemoautotrophic organisms, therefore, provide a rich food source in a totally dark environment. They enable large communities of marine animals to live without ever receiving sunlight.

Giant Worms and Clams

Scientific questions about how vent colonies flourished did not end with the recognition of chemosynthesizing bacteria. The giant tubeworms, some up to 5 feet (1½ m) long and 1½ inches (4 cm) thick, presented a problem for biologists. Now known as *Riftia,* these slinky

The typical seafloor (viewed here from the *Alvin*) is almost barren of life because food supply, such as plankton, is sparse or absent.

creatures have no mouth or gut and therefore lack any visible means of existing. Yet they thrive as some of the densest animal populations on earth, with 200 or more worms sometimes occupying an area the size of a baseball pitcher's mound.

Early examinations showed that *Riftia* are made of four major body parts. At the head end is a feathery plume that protrudes from the tube. The plumes are red because their thin individual filaments have blood inside. A collarlike structure surrounds the plume, and this is attached to the trunk which makes up about 75 percent of the body length. At the base of the trunk is a structure that anchors the worm to rocky seafloor.

High-powered microscopy helped explain how tube worms survive. Each plume filament contains vessels that circulate blood between the worm's body and the filament tips. The plumes, biologists

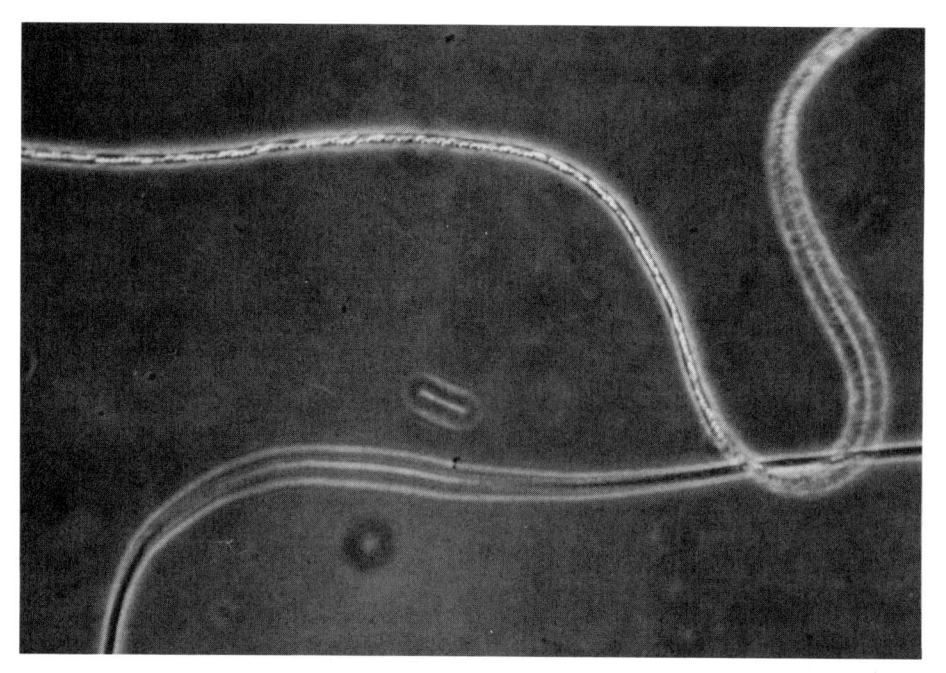

The threadlike bacteria *Beggiatoa,* as seen through a microscope, has helped scientists understand how life survives without sunlight.

learned, serve as exchange organs for the intake of oxygen and hydrogen sulfide from the seawater and for the removal of wastes.

More surprising to biologists was that tissue inside the worm's trunk is composed of large amounts of bacteria. The bacteria survive and grow through chemosynthesis that forms organic carbon. Additionally, some of this bacterial carbon finds its way into the worm's body, enabling the mouthless and gutless *Riftia* to obtain most of its nutrients from microscopic "guests." There is a symbiotic relationship between the two animals, meaning that each offers a means of support to the other.

But there is a dangerous flip-side to this relationship. Sulfide is a poison. If an animal allows sulfide to enter its body to nourish symbiont, or co-existing bacteria, it risks self-poisoning. As defenses,

These tubeworms share their habitat in the northeast Pacific Ocean, near Washington State, with a seafloor mat of bacteria.

however, *Riftia* has developed a sulfide-binding protein in its blood that enables the proper balance between providing sulfide to its bacteria and preventing self-contamination. Tubeworms also have special enzymes in their sausagelike body walls where blood supply is thin. These enzymes are a peripheral defense that oxidizes sulfide entering its cells to render it harmless.

Giant vent clams, too, are symbiotic with bacteria. Chemoautotrophic bacteria occupy clam gills and provide enough nourishment for the shelled animals to reach 10 inches (25 cm) in length, the size of some clams living in shallow sunlit waters.

In some cases, rapid and large clam-shell growth can be hazardous to tubeworms. When the Rose Garden in the Pacific Ocean between the Galapagos Islands and Ecuador was revisited in 1985—five years

A cluster of tubeworms on the Pacific floor near the Galapagos Islands.

after the first visit in the *Alvin*—investigators noted a comparatively sharp decrease in tubeworms and an increase in clams and mussels. Also, many of the remaining worms were no longer erect but instead were bent over as though seeking better contact with water jetting from cracks. The most likely reason for these changes was a decrease in vent flow. While worms require strong, steady streams of hydrothermal solutions passing over them to deliver nutrients, clams and mussels survive by planting their foot into a crack to extract nutrients from the exiting warm water. With too many shelled animals occupying cracks, water flow became restricted and the tube worms suffered.

In order to determine how rapidly vent clams can grow, scientists analyze their shells for naturally radioactive elements such as radium, thorium, and uranium. Dr. Karl Turekian at Yale University calculated that vent clams from one part of the East Pacific rise grow from 1.5 to 2.5 inches (4 to 6 cm) per year and those from another part grow about ¼ inch (½ cm) per year. According to Turekian's studies, these growth rates are from 70 to 700 times faster than those of shell animals on ordinary cold and dark seafloor. Growth-rate studies also indicate that vent clams reach ages of about twenty years, a life span similar to that of shallow-water clams. Most growth, however, occurs in the earliest years.

The clams, bacteria, and giant worms have caught most of the attention from those who study vent biology, but still other life forms coexist in the submarine warmth. Sieving the soft sediments and examining the scrapings of clam shells have turned up numerous varieties of worms and single-shelled snail-like animals. Exactly what types of animals and bacteria make up a vent colony depends largely on water temperatures, food supply, and which animals successfully migrated there from other hydrothermal vents.

Starting New Colonies

Because vents are seafloor "oases" of life, often separated by hundreds of miles of near-freezing water, marine biologists question how marine life locates new ones to colonize. Some solutions to this mystery come from studying the earliest growth stages, or larval shells, of bivalved (two-shelled) colony members such as clams. Studies of shallow-water (sunlit) larval shells—largely done by electron microscopy because they are smaller than 1 mm—indicate two early-growth types. One is planktotrophic, meaning that the larvae can feed during their free-swimming stage and therefore travel great distances in currents. Other larvae are nonplanktotrophic and depend for nutrition on the yolk of their egg. This limits the distances of free swimming and relocation because the available nutrients are eventually consumed.

Planktotrophic larvae are present as hydrothermal vents. They may drift in the water column for several weeks or even months before locating a new warm vent to colonize. Water currents can move 10 inches (25 cm) per second, enabling larval shells to travel hundreds of miles before locating a new warm vent to colonize.

It is not clear, however, how the nonplanktotrophic clam larvae living at hydrothermal vents relocate to colonize new vents. In one example on the East Pacific rise, 2,000 miles (3,300 km) separate vent fields that house several varieties of clams that have nonplanktotrophic larvae. One possible explanation for the dispersal of larvae that do not take food from seawater is that migration in the extreme cold slows their need to utilize nutrients in their egg yolk.

A Long History

However new life populates warm springs as they sprout up on the midocean ridge system, studies of some rock formations on land indicate that none of the populations are new to the earth. For example, the Samail ophiolite in the Middle Eastern country of Oman represents fragments of oceanic crust thrust onto a continental margin about 100 million years ago. Massive sulfide deposits near the top of this geologic structure indicate that the ophiolite represents a spreading center on an ancient seafloor. Moreover, the vent had been colonized.

In January 1983, Dr. Rachel Haymon of the University of California at Santa Barbara and Dr. Randolph Koski of the U.S. Geological Survey entered an underground copper mine in northern Oman to study and compare the ancient sulfide deposits with those at hydrothermal vents. When examining zinc sulfide samples, they discovered that some of the mineralized rock had tubular structures 1 to 5 mm in length. These fossil tubes were almost identical to tube structures known to be made by worms at vents along the East Pacific rise. Accordingly, the Oman worm tubes were proof that hydrothermal vents have formed throughout a long period of geologic time, produced metal deposits, became colonized, and eventually expired.

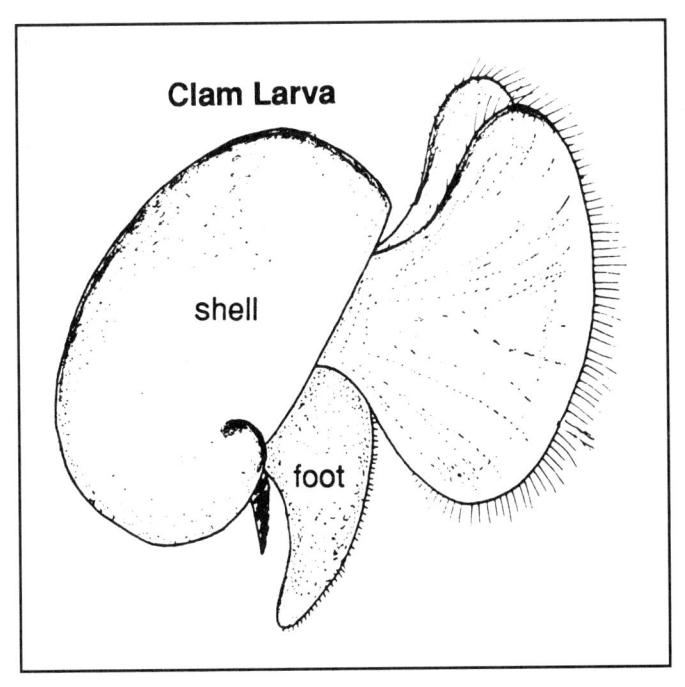

This is an example of the earliest growth stage of a clam.

Discoveries such as fossil worm tubes give scientists new perspectives on how the earth works from geologic, biologic, and chemical points of view. Continued studies of hydrothermal vents assure more insight into the earth—not only for better understanding its past, but also for identifying future resources and for achieving a cleaner environment by applying some of the chemical processes observed at vents.

5

Black Smokers and the Science Ahead

According to the concept of plate tectonics, no part of the ocean floor is older than about 250 million years—even though the earth is over four billion years old. The reason is that oceans existing before 250 million years ago have since closed from collisions between moving plates of lithosphere. In general, then, the earth's earliest oceans were destroyed and lost—unless the closing of an ocean included buckling portions of ocean floor up onto land. New oceans have always formed, however, because continuous shifting of the earth's plates breaks continents apart. The Atlantic Ocean, for example, is less than 200 million years old, filling in the gap when North America separated from Europe and northwest Africa.

Fortunately for geologists, remnants of some ancient oceans are available on continents for scientific examination. In one example, rocks exposed in the Isua area at the edge of the ice cap in western Greenland are among the oldest known by geologists. Special dating techniques that utilize radioactive elements in rocks indicate that Isua rocks are 3.75 billion years old, or formed at a time when the earth was less than one billion years old.

Earliest Life?

The Isua rocks have undergone physical and chemical changes over their long existence in the earth's crust but still contain clues to where and how they originated. They are largely silica-rich rocks formed in seawater, volcanic rocks of the type making up ocean floors today, and ironstone. Accordingly, geologists who specialize in interpreting the earth's most ancient rocks believe that the Isua area of Greenland represents one of the earliest seafloor hydrothermal systems.

If hydrothermal vents have operated since before life began, affecting the chemical compositions of the oceans, scientists wonder if early vents influenced the chemical reactions that led to life's origin. A particular feature of the Isua rocks sheds light on this subject. The rocks appear to contain microscopic fossils of one-celled biologic structures. The simplicity of these ancient life forms and the old age

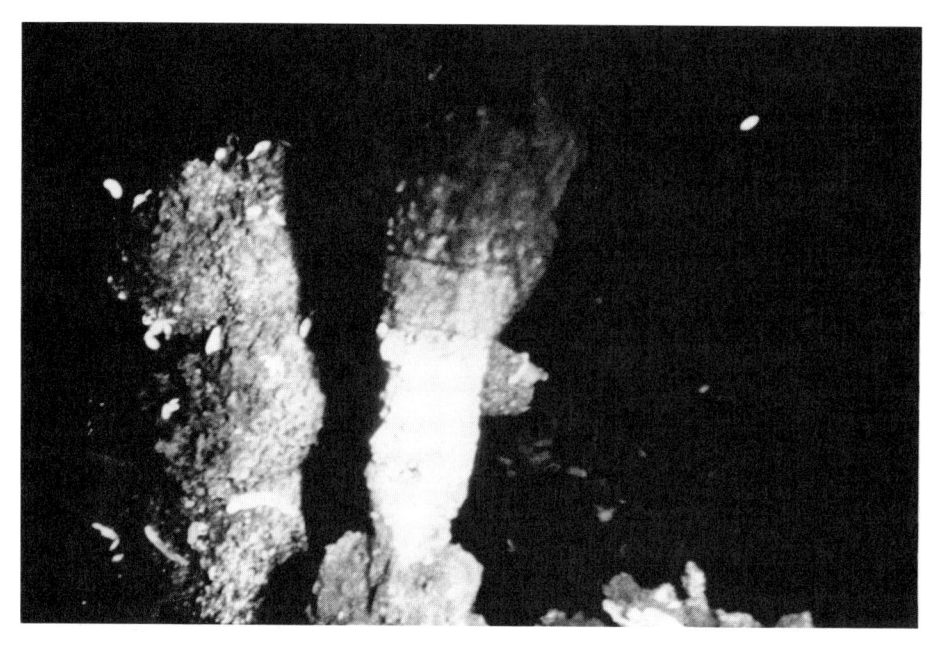

Black smokers like these on the East Pacific rise may have been active in the earth's earliest oceans several billions of years ago.

of the rocks suggests to some scientists the discovery of the earliest occurrences of life on earth.

To Dr. John Corliss of Oregon State University, among the first geologists to view a hydrothermal vent from *Alvin*, the Isua rocks indicate that life on earth began at seafloor vents. Dr. Corliss and colleagues J. A. Baross and S. E. Hoffman proposed that hydrothermal vents provided the necessary ingredients and conditions, such as hydrogen sulfide and methane gases, metals, heat, and rising watery solutions, to create life from nonliving matter. These researchers see the vents as manufacturers of the building blocks of life, amino acids, and incubators for changing amino acids into living cells that survived and grew as chemoautotrophs.

On the other hand, University of California at San Diego chemists S. L. Miller and J. L. Bada do not agree. They explain in an August 1988 issue of the British science journal *Nature* that the temperatures at hydrothermal vents were probably too hot for early life to form and survive there. And E. G. Nisbit of the University of Saskatchewan in Canada warns against possible misinterpretation of organic remains in rocks thought to represent ancient hydrothermal fields. The forms thought to be fossils of early life may after all be nonbiologic features, or pseudofossils.

Another problem with accepting hydrothermal vents as the places where life began is that seafloor environments, as we know them, are rich in oxygen. And the only way oxygen could be present in large amounts at vents, or anywhere on earth, is from photosynthesis. In other words, life had to have existed somewhere on earth before vent life could thrive. Perhaps, then, life forms at early vents were different from what we observe, developing and living in the absence of oxygen. At the moment, the problem of exactly how hydrothermal vents fit into the origin of life remains unsolved.

Methane Gives Life
If the origin of life is associated with hydrothermal systems, what does

this indicate about possible life on other planets? Certainly other planets have not had the same geologic history as the earth, where plate tectonics and ocean basins enabled hydrothermal vents to form. Could amino acids and simple cells of life develop under other conditions? A 1984 *Alvin* dive to 2 miles (3¼ km) in the Gulf of Mexico helps answer that question.

In an expedition to study underwater erosion off the west coast of Florida, an *Alvin* party headed by Dr. Charles Paull of Scripps Institution of Oceanography unexpectedly found communities of tubeworms, large shelled animals, and bacterial mats. Knowing that there was no hot water or magma in this region of the earth's crust, the scientists pondered why and how organisms like those of hydrothermal vents lived in the dark of the cold Gulf of Mexico seafloor.

Dark, columnar structures in ancient rocks, such as the stromatolites in this 2.7 billion year old rock from Canada, can be misinterpreted as organic remains of early life. The scale bar is 1 cm; sample is a wafer of rock mounted on a glass slide and viewed through a microscope that transmits light through the slide.

The presence of supersaline waters, sulfide minerals, and nearby seafloor limestone suggested that the production of acids and hydrogen sulfide seeping from the seafloor were responsible for providing life. That is, once again, chemosynthesis by bacteria was thought to be the main reason for this marine life in the dark. Only this time there was no heat, which indicated that nutrients are more important than warmth for large-shell life and worm life to colonize.

After the discovery and study of other non-vent communities of large shells and worms in the Gulf of Mexico—such as one offshore from Louisiana—and another in a subduction zone off Oregon, scientists obtained more details about how these colonies survive in cold (non-vent) waters. It appears that seepage of methane gas, probably from underlying petroleum (hydrocarbon) concentrations, provides the source of the carbon needed to sustain some marine life. By methane's

Large clams gather where oil seeps (dark area) from rocks on the floor of the Gulf of Mexico.

entering seawater and being utilized by bacteria, such as those residing in the gills of clams, certain life forms have become methylotrophic (methane-using). Perhaps, then, a cold planet that seeps methane could also support life. Methane-rich Neptune, examined in the late 1980s by the *Voyager 2* spacecraft, is such a candidate.

Enriching Our Lives

Our understanding of sulfide-eating bacteria at seafloor vents has applications in society. One of the by-products of industry is the release of sulfur compounds into the atmosphere that can later return as acid rain to damage lakes and streams. Some methods being investigated to reduce this environmental hazard include using chemosynthetic bacteria to convert industrial hydrogen sulfide into harmless forms of sulfur that can be diluted in the oceans.

This field of biotechnology—sometimes referred to as genetic engineering—is expanding rapidly. The Department of the Interior, for example, funds research to develop bacteria that remove the sulfur from coal. Private industry, such as Canadian Giant Bay Resources, is treating gold-bearing sulfurous rocks with bacteria that use sulfur as an energy source. They break down the structure of the rocks so that extracting gold becomes easier.

These experiments are tied to the biologic knowledge acquired from hydrothermal vent systems. The most direct geologic benefit from vents, however, would be to mine the metals. Scientists have no doubt that billions of dollars in minerals are locked in hydrothermal vents, such as the 5 ounces (140 g) of gold estimated for each ton of rock at the Sea Cliff hydrothermal field offshore from Oregon. This metal resource is within the United States' Exclusive Economic Zone and therefore politically suitable for the United States to mine. But the Department of the Interior's Mineral Management Service has no intention of leasing mineral rights—or permission to mine—in the near future.

Certain practical problems must be solved before efforts are made to recover metal. One of the main concerns expressed during the 1988 annual meeting of the Underwater Mining Institute—a committee of industry, research, and government officials—was that developing the technological know-how to mine vents is a large obstacle to recovering ore. For example, a U.S. Department of the Interior panel on marine engineering concluded that there is little or no technology available today for mining in water of 100 to 10,000 feet (30 to 3,000 m) deep. What could be valuable ore, then, remains worthless. Minerals have no economic value if they are not recoverable.

One reason that governments and private industry are slow to develop the means to mine the seafloor is cost. In addition to the expense of developing the mining equipment, there is the cost of operating it far from land and in water depths of about two miles. Significant, too, is the metals market. The amount of money that metals bring changes with supply and demand. When a metal is needed badly, as for communications wiring or for national security, or if a metal is scarce, it can bring a high price. On the other hand, the price for a metal falls when demand is low or when supply is great. For the most part, the principal metals of hydrothermal vents—copper, iron, and zinc—are abundant on land and can be mined relatively cheaply.

Strengthening the Sciences

As it stands, then, the best use for the metals of hydrothermal vents is for research and learning. This is probably best, too, for the animal colonies. Many of the species of vent worms, clams, and bacteria are not found elsewhere on earth. Scientists are just now learning how these communities survive and reproduce in their hostile undersea habitats. If they are disturbed by mining, the world is liable to lose rare marine animals and valuable knowledge about them from environmental damage.

Hydrothermal vents are also proving useful for attracting new students, from grade-school through college ages, to careers in ocean and earth sciences. One approach has been to use the robotic, unmanned submersible *Jason* to explore and transmit video pictures of submarine geysers on the flank of Mount Vesuvius located 100 miles (160 km) from Naples, Italy. The satellite hookup of the telecasts provided science museums with live presentations for school children to view and introduced them to submarine geology and technology. Project *Jason* is intended to encourage young people's interest in science.

Dr. Susan E. Humphris, the dean of the Sea Education Association, a nonprofit organization in Woods Hole, Massachusetts, has another approach to exciting young people about ocean research. She recruits university students to include a semester of their schooling at sea. The SEA college-credit program combines six weeks of oceanographic instruction in the classroom, including topics on hydrothermal vents, with excursions on one of two oceangoing vessels. On board and at

Recycling metal, such as by shredding automobiles in scrapyards, is far cheaper than mining new metal from the seafloor.

sea in the Atlantic Ocean, students perform scientific experiments on water temperatures, salinity, and currents and learn to sample and study sea life. Over two thousand students have sailed with Sea Semester on the vessels *Westward* and *Cramer*. Many have gone on to specialize in marine science studies elsewhere, and some are certain to become researchers of hydrothermal vents.

The discovery of hydrothermal vents is one of this century's great finds. The information that the vents and their animal kingdoms have provided in only ten years has given many new ideas and facts to the sciences of geology, biology, oceanography, and chemistry. Left to survive in the dark, with only occasional visits by submersibles, these oddities of the world will continue to enlighten humankind with the riches of scientific information.

The *Cramer* (left) and the *Westward* (right) vessels are used by oceanography students in the university program operated by the Sea Education Association, Woods Hole, Massachusetts.

Glossary

amino acids—a group of organic compounds that are the building blocks of life; amino acids combine to form proteins.

biology—the science that studies living organisms, particularly their origin, development, structure, and reproduction.

chemoautotrophic—utilizing an inorganic substance as a source of energy.

chemosynthesis—synthesis of organic material such as carbon by energy derived from chemical reactions.

crust—outermost layer of the earth; oceanic crust is about 5 miles (8 km) thick, and continental crust is about 30 miles (50 km) thick.

geology—the study of the earth, its material, and the processes that act upon the earth.

geyser—a hot spring that forcibly ejects hot water and steam into the air; the heat results from groundwater seeping close to a magma reservoir in the subsurface.

heterotrophic—obtaining nourishment from outside sources that obtain energy by photosynthesis; animals eating photosynthetic plants are an example.

hotspot—a localized portion of the earth emitting more than normal amounts of heat from great depths within the earth, usually enough heat to cause volcanism.

hot spring—a spring whose waters are above normal surface temperatures owing to warming by magma beneath the surface.

hydrothermal solutions—hot fluids, largely water, moving in the crust and ejected from a vent in the crust, sometimes having temperatures above the boiling point of water.

hydrothermal vent—a vent ejecting a stream of hot, or hydrothermal, solutions.

larva—the early form of any animal that is unlike its parent and must pass through stages of growth before assuming adult characteristics.

lava—magma, or molten rock, that has reached the surface.

lithosphere—the outer, rigid shell of the earth, about 60 miles (100 km) thick and containing the earth's crust.

magma—molten rock; magma forms igneous rock upon cooling.

massive sulfides—large accumulations of sulfur- and metal-bearing minerals, such as zinc sulfide (the mineral sphalerite).

methane—an odorless, flammable gas that is lighter than air and occurs naturally as a product of decomposition of organic matter.

methylotrophic—obtaining energy from methane.

midocean ridge—a mountainous (largely volcanic rock) linear feature of the seafloor marking the boundary between two lithospheric plates.

mineral—a naturally occurring solid material with definite chemical and physical properties, including a crystalline structure; table salt, or halite, is an example.

oasis—an isolated fertile area surrounded by barrenness.

oceanography—the study of the oceans.

ophiolite—an assemblage of rocks that represent the ocean crust thrust upon land.

photoautotrophic—obtaining energy from light.

photosynthesis—synthesis of compounds such as carbon with the aid of light in chlorophyll-containing cells; plant life grows and survives by this biologic process.

plankton—small animals and plants floating or weakly swimming in a body of water.

spreading center—a region of the lithosphere marked by the boundary between two plates that are spreading apart from one another; usually marked by a mid-ocean ridge.

subduction—the passing of one lithospheric plate beneath another at a region of the earth where two plates collide.

submersible—a small submarine used for underwater research, capable of transporting about three people from sea level to the ocean floor.

sulfide minerals—minerals that contain sulfur combined with a metal; *also see* massive sulfides.

symbiosis—the living together by two or more organisms of different types that need each other to survive.

vent—a vertical outlet in the crust through which hot gases, liquids, and magma may pass.

warm spring—*see* hot spring.

Further Reading

Ballard, R.D., "Exploring the East Pacific Rise," *Oceanus* v. 27, no. 3, p. 7-14, 1984.

Corliss, J.B., Baross, J.A., and Hoffman, S.E., "An hypothesis concerning the relationship between submarine hot springs and the origin of life on earth," *Oceanologica Acta* v. 4, Supplement Paper p. 56-69, 1981.

Edmond, J.M., and Von Damm, K., "Hot springs on the ocean floor," *Scientific American* v. 248, no. 4, p. 78-93, 1983.

Edmond, J.M., "The geochemistry of ridge crest hot springs," *Oceanus* v. 27, no. 3, p. 15-19, 1984.

Fodor, R.V., *Gold, Copper, Iron: How Metals Are Formed, Found, and Used,* Enslow Publishers, Inc., Hillside, NJ, 1989.

Fodor, R.V., *Earth in Motion: The Concept of Plate Tectonics.* William Morrow and Co., New York, 1978.

Haymon, R.M., and Macdonald, K.C., "The geology of deep-sea hot springs," *American Scientist* v. 73, p. 441-449, 1985.

Hekinian, R., Fevrier, Bischoff, J.L., Picot, P., Shanks W.C., "Sulfide deposits from the East Pacific rise near 21° N," *Science* v. 207, p. 1433-1444.

Jannasch, H.W., "Chemosynthesis: the nutritional basis for life at deep-sea vents," *Oceanus* v. 27, no. 3, p. 73-78, 1984.

Jones, M.L., "The giant tube worms," *Oceanus* v. 27, no. 3, p. 47-53, 1984.

Jones, M.L. (editor), "Hydrothermal vents of the eastern Pacific: an overview," *Bulletin of the Biological Society of Washington,* no. 6, INFAX Corp., Vienna, Virginia, 1985.

Karl, D.M., McMurtry, G.M., Malahoff, A., and Garcia, M.O., "Loihi seamount, Hawaii: a mid-plate volcano with a distinctive hydrothermal system," *Nature* v. 335, p. 532-534, 1988.

Kennicutt, M.C., Brooks, J.M., Bidigare, R.R., and Denoux, G.J., "Gulf of Mexico hydrocarbon seep communities. I. Regional distribution of hydrocarbon seepage and associated fauna." *Deep Sea Research* v. 35, p. 1639-1651, 1988.

Koski, R.A., Normark, W.R., Morton, J.L., and Delaney, J.R., "Metal sulfide deposits on the Juan de Fuca Ridge," *Oceanus* v. 25, no. 3, p. 42-48, 1982.

Meyerson, A. Lee, *Seawater: A Delicate Balance*. Hillside, NJ: Enslow Publishers, 1988.

Miller, S.L., and Bada, J.L., "Submarine hot springs and the origin of life," *Nature* v. 334, p. 609-611, 1988.

Mottl, M.J., "Submarine hydrothermal ore deposits," *Oceanus* v. 23, no. 2, p. 18-27, 1980.

Rona, P.A. (editor), *Hydrothermal Process at Seafloor Spreading Centers*, Plenum Press, New York, 1983.

Rona, P.A., "Hydrothermal mineralization at seafloor spreading centers," *Earth Science Reviews*, v. 20, p. 1-104, 1984.

Rona, P.A., "Mineral deposits from sea-floor hot springs," *Scientific American* v. 254, no. 1, p. 84-92, 1986.

Index

A
Alexander the Great, 12
Alvin, the, 5-9, 25, 27, 29, 35, 45, 51-52
amino acids, 52
Aristotle, 11

B
bacteria, 40-44, 52-54
Beebe, William, 12

C
Challenger, the H. M. S., 11
chemosynthesis, 40-41, 53
chimneys, rock, 8, 9, 10, 21-25, 28, 33-36
clams, giant, 7, 27, 44-45
 growth rate, 45, 47
colonizing vents, 45-46

E
earthquakes, 20
East Pacific rise, 18-19, 26-27, 35
echo sounder, 11

F
Fulton, Robert, 12

G
Galapagos Islands, 5, 7, 18, 44
geysers, 22

H
Hawaiian Islands, 23-24
Helgafell volcano, 15-*17*
hotspots, 23-24
hydrogen sulfide, 8, 40-41, 43, 51, 54
hydrothermal
 field, 23, 28-29, 51, 54
 solutions, 21, 23-24, 26-27, 29-30, 33-34, 36, 45
 vents, 8-12, 14, 22-25, 28, 47, 50-52, 55, 57

I
Iceland, 15-17, 20

K
Knorr, the, 5, 8

L
larval shells, 46-47
lava, 15-18, 24
lithosphere, 19-20
Loihi submarine volcano, *24-25*

M

magma, 18-23
metal deposits, 10, 14, 25, 27-29, 32-33, 47, 54-55
methane, 51, 53-54
Mid-Atlantic Ridge, 17, *19*
midocean ridge system, 17-18, 20-22, 23, 26, 33, 46
minerals, definition, 31-32
mineral deposits, 30, 35-36
mining vents, 54-55

P

photosynthesis, 38-40, 51
plankton, 39-*40*
plates, 19, 21
plate tectonics, 14, 19-20, 49, 52

S

Sea Cliff, the, 13, 29-*30*
Sea Education Association, 56-57
smokers, 10, 13, 20-21, 27, 35, 50
"spreading center," 20
stromatolites, *52*
subduction, 20-21, 53
sulfide minerals, 27-28, 31, 33-35, 43-44, 46-47, 53
Surtsey Island, 16

T

Trieste, the, 12

tubeworms, 8, 27, 41, 42,*43-44*, 45, 52
fossilized, 47-48
symbiotic relationship with, 44

V

vent lifeforms, 6-8, 10-12, 14, 27-28, 36, 39-40, 52
vent temperatures, 5, 8-9, 21, 23, 32-33, 36, 51
volcanism, 20